Making Dolls

by Carol Nicklaus

an easy-read ACTIVITY book

Franklin Watts
New York | London | Toronto | Sydney
1981

G
A GROLIER COMPANY

R.L.   3.1   Spache Revised Formula

Library of Congress Cataloging in Publication Data

Nicklaus, Carol.
  Making dolls.

  (An Easy-read activity book)
  Summary: Provides instructions for making dolls from
pipe cleaners, yarn, paper, and other common items.
    1. Dollmaking—Juvenile literature.   [1. Dollmaking.
2. Handicraft]   I. Title.   II. Series: Easy-read activity
book.
TT175.N48   745.592'21   81-709
ISBN 0-531-04309-6   AACR2

CONTENTS

MATERIALS	5
CLOTHES-PEG DOLLS	6
PIPE CLEANER DOLLS	8
SPOOL DOLL	10
YARN DOLLS	12
HAND PUPPET DOLL	16
ROLY-POLY DOLL	18
PAPER DOLLS	20
BEANBAG BABY DOLL	22
CLOTH DOLL	24
FACES FOR YOUR DOLLS	28
HAIR FOR YOUR DOLLS	29
DRESSING UP YOUR DOLLS	30

C I

Children and dolls have always been friends. You probably already have a doll you like. Did you ever want to make a doll yourself? This book will show you how. It's fun!

You can make dolls to play with, or make one to give to a little brother or sister or to a friend.

Don't worry if your doll is not exactly like the ones in this book. You can make them just the way you want. Every doll is a little different, just like real people, and that's why a doll you make is special.

MATERIALS

You may already have at home most of the things you will need to make these dolls. When you decide which one you want to make, read all the instructions first. Get together everything you will need. You might want to ask a grown-up to help you find some of the materials to use, or to answer any questions you have.

When you finish making your doll, be sure to clean up your brushes and paints, and put your materials away. That way everything will be ready when you want to make another doll.

CLOTHES-PEG DOLLS

Clothes-peg dolls are easy to make. Plain clothes-pegs look a little bit like dolls already, don't they?

YOU WILL NEED:
wooden clothes-pegs
scraps of fabric
construction paper

brushes and acrylic paints
   or waterproof marking pens
pipe cleaners
white glue

The round part of the clothes-peg will be your doll's head. Draw or paint a face on the front of the head, and paint hair on the top and back. Paint the body of the doll to look like anyone you want. Look at the pictures for some ideas.

6

Twist a pipe cleaner around the neck of your doll to make two arms.

To make a dress for your doll, cut out a piece of fabric that looks like this:

Wrap it around under the arms of the doll and glue it in place.

To make an angel's wings, cut out a piece of white or yellow construction paper shaped like this:

Glue the wings to the back of your doll. When the glue is dry, bend the wings back a little bit.

You could make lots and lots of clothes-peg dolls, and each one would look a little different.

PIPE CLEANER DOLLS

Pipe cleaner dolls are fun to play with because you can bend them into different positions. You can pretend they are doing almost anything!

YOU WILL NEED:

pipe cleaners
yarn
cotton balls

white glue
brushes and acrylic paints
   or waterproof marking pens

Twist two pipe cleaners to make one long one. Bend this to make the doll's head and body. Look at the pictures to see how.

Twist another pipe cleaner around the doll's neck to make arms. Add two more near the bottom of the body for the legs and feet.

Stuff a cotton ball inside the loop of the doll's head, and put one or two in the loop for the body. Now wrap the yarn all around the doll. Wrap and wrap until the whole doll is covered. This will take a long time! Tuck in the last end of the yarn and glue it to the doll's body.

Draw or paint a face on the front of the doll's head. Cut small pieces of yarn and sew or glue them on the doll's head for hair.

You can make clothes for pipe cleaner dolls. Look at pages 30, 31, and 32 for some ideas.

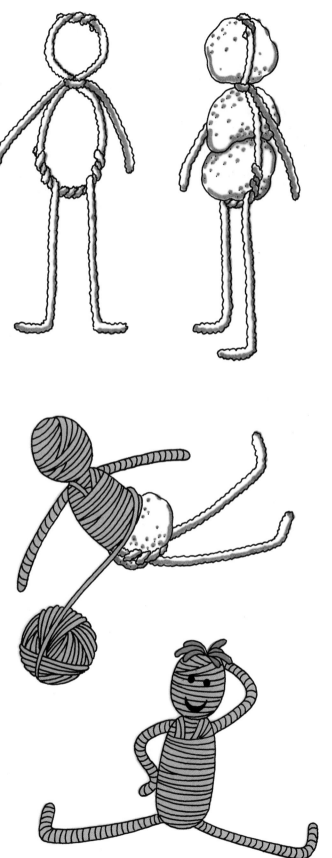

SPOOL DOLL

A spool doll is floppy and wiggly. Tie a piece of elastic to the top of his head and watch him dance!

YOU WILL NEED:
a spool for the head
a larger spool for the body
three shoelaces

buttons with large loops
** for hands and feet**
brushes and acrylic paints
** or waterproof marking pens**

Take off any paper labels on the spools. Draw or paint a face on one side of the smaller spool, and paint a design on the larger one.

10

Thread one shoelace down through the smaller spool, then through the larger one. Leave a loop at the bottom of the larger spool. Then thread the shoelace back up through both spools.

Put another shoelace through the loop, and tie it in a big knot in the middle. These are the legs. Pull the threaded shoelace tight and tie it in a knot at the top of the doll's head.

Tie a third shoelace between the spools for arms.

Tie buttons on the ends of his arms and legs, for hands and feet. Cut the shoelaces if they look too long. Now he's ready to dance!

11

YARN DOLLS

Yarn dolls are soft and cuddly, and babies love
to hug them.

YOU WILL NEED:
acrylic knitting yarn
buttons or felt for eyes, nose, and mouth
needle and thread
scissors
transparent tape
a piece of heavy cardboard
   about 9 by 12 inches (22.9 by 30.5 cm)

Tape one end of your
yarn to the bottom of
the piece of cardboard.
Then wrap the yarn
around the cardboard
the long way lots and
lots of times. Be careful
not to pull it too tight.
The more you wrap, the
fatter your doll will be.

12

When you have enough, cut the end of the yarn and tape it to the cardboard.

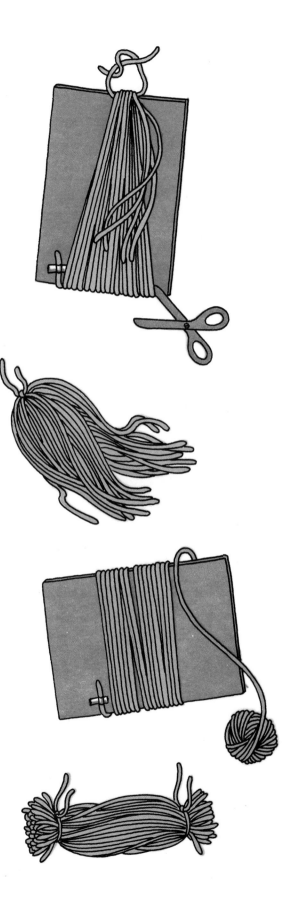

Cut another piece of yarn about 8 inches (20.3 cm) long and slide it under the bunch of yarn. Pull it to the top and tie it in a square knot as tightly as you can. Cut through all the yarn at the bottom, and take it off the cardboard.

Wrap some more yarn around the cardboard the short way. Cut this yarn at both ends, and take it off the cardboard. Then tie each end together.

Tie a piece of yarn in a knot around the big bunch, about 2 inches (5.1 cm) from the top. Now you can see the doll's head.

To make arms, put the small bunch across right under the neck, in the middle of the big bunch.

Tie another piece of yarn very tightly right under the arms. If you want a doll who looks like she's wearing a long skirt, you are finished already!

To make legs, divide the bunch of yarn in half below the doll's waist. Tie yarn around each leg to make feet. Trim any extra-long ends that are sticking out.

Cut out eyes, a nose, and a mouth from felt, and sew them on the doll's face. Or sew on buttons for eyes.

You might want to tie a ribbon around your doll's neck for a necktie. Or tie ribbon around its middle for a belt.

Now give your doll a big hug!

HAND PUPPET DOLL

Here is a doll you can wear on your hand.

YOU WILL NEED:
an old fabric or knit glove
    that fits your hand
a plain, hollow rubber ball
    about 3 inches (7.6 cm) in diameter
acrylic paints and brushes
    or waterproof marking pens
white glue
a curly metal or plastic pad for scrubbing
    dishes (the kind without soap!)
fabric scraps and buttons
needle and thread
scissors

Ask a grown-up to help you cut a hole in the rubber ball. Make the hole big enough to fit over the ends of three of your fingers. Paint a face on one side of the rubber ball.

16

Pull on the scrubbing pad until it is nice and loose. Glue it to the top and back of the rubber ball. This will make hair for your doll.

To make a skirt, cut a piece of fabric like this: Make it long enough to fit around the glove two times. Sew the short edges together. Sew a thread loosely all around the top of the skirt. Then pull it so that the fabric gathers. Fit the skirt around the glove, and sew it on. Sew two buttons to the palm side of the glove.

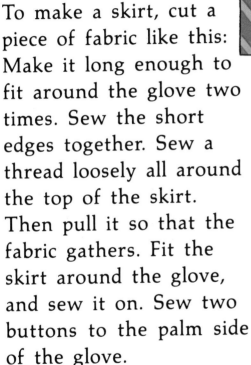

Put your hand inside the glove. Put the rubber ball over your first three fingers, and there she is. Can you make her wave hello?

17

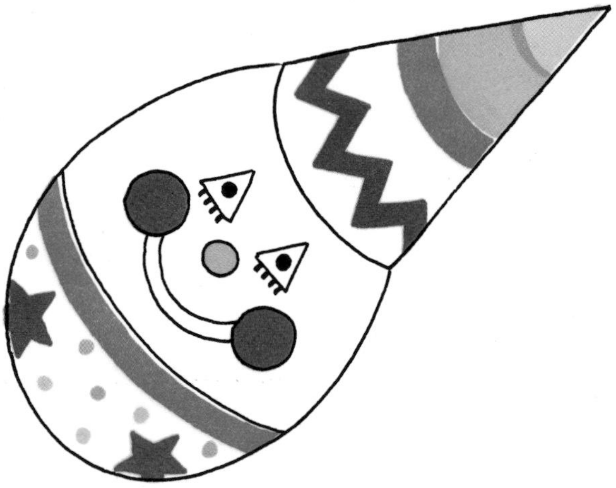

ROLY-POLY DOLL

This silly doll never falls over and never stands up straight!

YOU WILL NEED:

a plastic egg-shaped container
brushes and acrylic paints
or waterproof marking pens
clay
white glue or decorated tape
construction paper
scissors

The larger half of the egg will be the doll's head. The smaller half will be the body. Paint or draw a funny face on the front of the top half and a bright clown suit on the bottom.

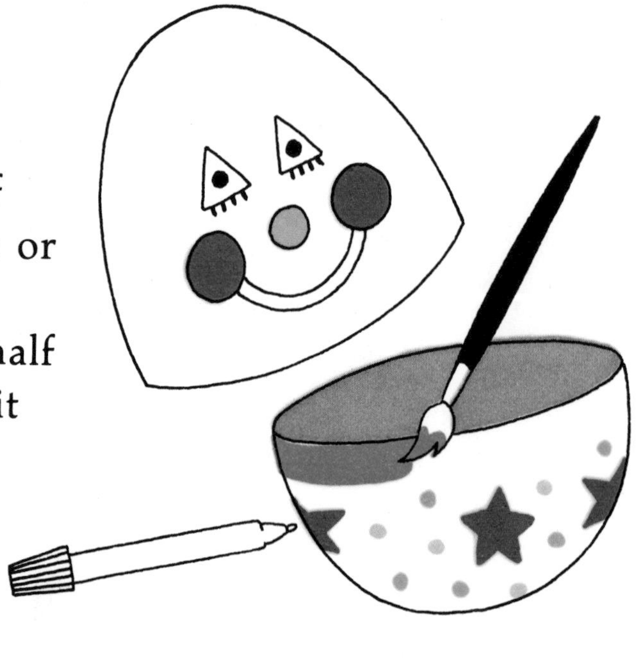

Stick some clay inside the middle of the bottom half. Put in enough so that the doll stands up when the top is on.

Put the two halves of the egg together. Use glue or the tape to hold the edges together.

To make a hat for your doll, cut out a half-circle shape from construction paper like this:

Put a design on it. Bend it into a cone, and tape or glue the edges together. Glue the hat to the top of the doll's head.

Now just try to knock the doll over!

PAPER DOLLS

❈

Here are two kinds of paper dolls to make.
You can make one that looks like you!

YOU WILL NEED:
lightweight cardboard
  (from a cereal box or file folder)
pencil and scissors
glue

a photograph of your face
acrylic paints and brushes
    or waterproof marking pens
paper fasteners

To make a paper doll
that looks like you, draw
an outline of your body,
something like this:

Cut out the picture of
your face. Glue it on the
head of the doll. Now
draw or paint clothes on
the body. You can make
yourself look like
anything you want.

Cut out the doll. Then cut out a shape that looks like this:

Make it about two-thirds as tall as your doll. Fold the shape on the dotted line. Glue the smaller part to the back of the doll. Now your doll can stand up by itself.

To make a paper doll with movable arms and legs, draw five shapes like these: one head and body, two arms, and two legs. Paint them and cut them out.

Use a sharp pencil or the point of your scissors to punch holes at the x's, and attach the arms and legs to the body with the paper fasteners.

You can trace around this paper doll to make lots of action pictures.

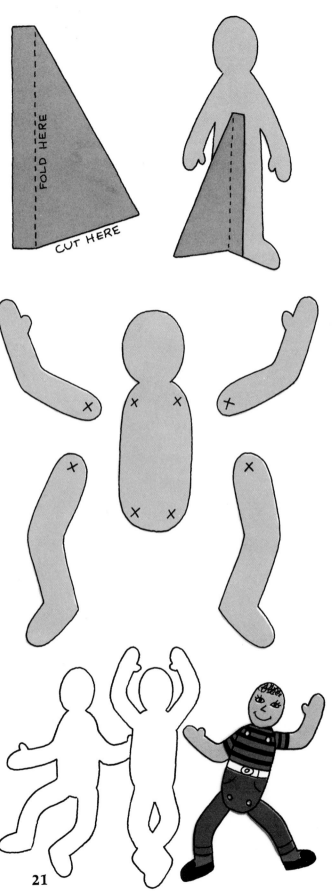

FOLD HERE

CUT HERE

21

BEANBAG BABY DOLL

You can play catch with the beanbag baby doll. She loves to bounce around!

YOU WILL NEED:

fabric
needle and thread
scissors

acrylic paints and brushes
   or waterproof marking pens
yarn
dry beans
safety pin

Cut out two pieces of fabric shaped like this:

Draw a face and arms on the front of one piece. Put the front sides of the fabric pieces facing each other together. Sew around the edges, following the dotted lines in the drawing. Leave an opening at the bottom. Turn the pieces right side out.

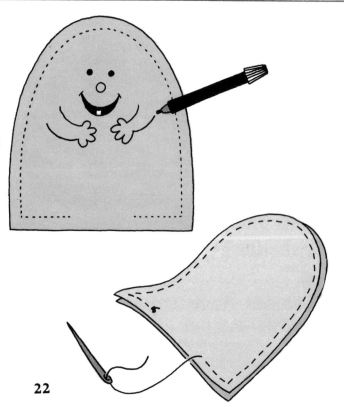

22

Fill the doll about two-thirds full with beans. Turn under the edges of the opening and sew it shut.

Tie a piece of yarn in a knot tightly around each of the bottom corners of the doll. This makes the legs.

Make some hair for your beanbag baby. Cut five or six pieces of yarn about 6 inches long (15.2 cm). Sew each one through the top of the doll's head. Tie them all together in a knot.

For the doll's diaper, cut out a piece of fabric shaped like this:
Fold it around the baby's bottom, and sew or pin it in place.

Now she's ready to play!

CUT OUT

CLOTH DOLL

You may want to ask a grown-up to help you sew this doll. You can make it any size you want, maybe even as big as you are!

YOU WILL NEED:
cardboard
fabric
needle and thread
yarn
acrylic paints
  or waterproof marking pens

cotton, foam rubber,
  or old stockings for stuffing
string

Draw a doll's shape like this on a piece of cardboard, and cut it out.

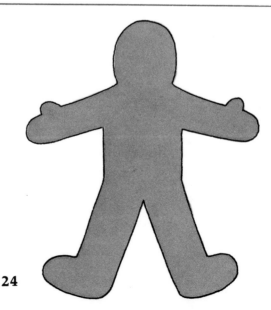

Trace the shape two times on the back side of the fabric, and cut out the pieces.

Draw or paint a face on the right side of one of the heads.

Put the right sides of the two shapes together and sew around the edges, following the dotted line in the picture. Leave an opening on one side of the body.

Turn the doll right side out, and put the stuffing inside. You can use the handle of a spoon to push the stuffing all the way to the ends of the arms and legs. When the doll is nice and plump, sew the opening shut.

Stitch through where the arms and legs join the body. This will make it easy for the arms and legs to move.

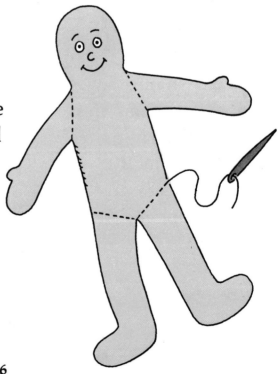

Wrap a piece of string around the doll's neck and tie it tightly in a square knot. This will help make the doll's head nice and round.

You can decorate your doll with paints or marking pens. Or, look at pages 30, 31, and 32 for ideas for making clothes for your doll. If your doll is big enough, he or she can even wear *your* clothes!

FACES FOR YOUR DOLLS

You will probably want to make a face on your doll. The face can be very simple, or it can look any way you want it to. Here are some ideas:

Make up a special face. It can be silly or sleepy or happy or even scary!

HAIR FOR YOUR DOLLS

Here are some ways to make hair for your doll. Hair can be long or short or straight or curly.

Cut yarn as long as you want and glue or sew it to your doll's head. You can make long hair and braid it for pigtails. Or pull the yarn apart so that it looks fuzzy.

You can glue on a piece of fur for hair, or make a beard or a moustache for your doll.

DRESSING UP YOUR DOLLS

Here are some ideas to help you dress up your dolls.

YOU WILL NEED:
fabric
needle and thread
paper

scissors
acrylic paints, crayons
    or waterproof marking pens

For a dress or shirt, cut out a piece of fabric that looks like this:
Make the piece twice as long as you want the dress or shirt to be. Be sure the hole in the middle is big enough to fit over your doll's head. Put the fabric over the doll, and tie it around the doll's waist.

CUT OUT

To make a pair of pants, cut two pieces of fabric like this:

Make them a little bigger than your doll's legs. Put the front sides of the fabric facing each other and sew the pieces together, following the dotted lines in the drawing.

Turn the pants right side out. Put them on your doll and tie them around the waist.

You can even draw clothes for your paper dolls. Trace a clothing shape around the doll's body and add tabs at the top.

Paint the clothes, and cut them out. Fold back the tabs so the clothes will hang on your doll's shoulders.

FOLD BACK

31

You can put lots of different decorations on your doll's clothes. Look around! Ask a grown-up to help you find some things you may use. Here are some ideas:

fabric scraps—cotton, velvet, corduroy, wool
  for patches or trim
old towels or blankets—for a robe or a coat
fur—for hats or collars
ribbons—for belts, neckties, or suspenders
lace—for collars, sleeves, or a hat
buttons
old jewelry and beads
pretend flowers